P. Holmes

TALES OUT OF SCHOOL

Made in Britain

by **David Leland**

Editor **Paul Kelley**
The Television Literacy Project

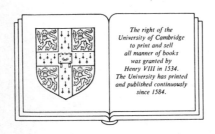

The right of the
University of Cambridge
to print and sell
all manner of books
was granted by
Henry VIII in 1534.
The University has printed
and published continuously
since 1584.

Cambridge University Press

Cambridge

London   New York   New Rochelle

Melbourne   Sydney

Tales out of School
Birth of a Nation
Flying into the Wind
Rhino
Made in Britain

Published by the Press Syndicate of the University of Cambridge
The Pitt Building, Trumpington Street, Cambridge CB2 1RP
32 East 57th Street, New York, NY 10022, USA
10 Stamford Road, Oakleigh, Melbourne 3166, Australia

First published 1986

Printed in Great Britain at the University Press, Cambridge

ISBN 0 521 31371 6

DS

Contents

A videocassette of this film is available to schools and colleges through the following British suppliers. (Please check for prices at the time of ordering.)

Concord Films Council Ltd
201 Felixstowe Road
Ipswich
Suffolk IP3 9BJ
(Videocassettes are also available for hire.)

The Guild Organisation Ltd
Guild House
Peterborough PE2 9PZ
(Videocassettes are also available for hire.)

Cambridge University Press
(Home Sales Department)
The Edinburgh Building
Shaftesbury Road
Cambridge CB2 2RU

Introduction

GILLER: *Then why are you here Trevor? There are those among us who would like to know the answer to that. And from where I'm standing it's not looking good.*

Scene 26

When I wrote the first draft of Made in Britain in 1981 I thought what held true for Trevor and his situation, also held true for many of the young people in this country, many of whom were in conflict with the law and authorities. Like the young people rioting in our streets, they are *Made in Britain*, products of our education system and our society as a whole. Being a covert optimist, I had hoped that things might change for the better.

But as time passes, I see few causes for optimism. People like Trevor would be no stranger to the events of recent months, and, I suspect, of the months to come. Fires are burning and people are dying in the streets of Handsworth, Brixton, Toxteth and Tottenham.

It is often said that there can be no excuses for the kind of behaviour witnessed in riots: there may not be any excuses, but there are plenty of reasons. Our society is littered with inequalities which, as the divisions grow, are passed down the line until they explode into violence on our streets.

A school teacher in Birmingham recently said to me, 'When the last lavatory stopped working, we had to send the children home.' This was a community school, deeply committed to the welfare of its pupils, where the teachers organise jumble sales and 'fun runs' to buy text books for its pupils. But economic hardship has caused them to sacrifice their educational principles until they were finally defeated by the plumbing. All this at a time when 2,000 additional cells for young people are included in the prison system's extensive rebuilding programme, and the manufacture of the instruments of oppression – riot equipment, water cannons, gas guns, plastic bullets, firearms – are enjoying an economic boom as government and police authorities spend, spend,

spend. Who is to mediate in this formula for conflict and destruction – and how?

Like any other child of five, Trevor first went to school with a natural, instinctive, inborn ability to enquire, explore and to learn. Also, like any other child, Trevor went on trust – trust in the judgement and will of parents, teachers and other adults. After eleven years, or fifteen thousand hours of compulsory schooling, what Trevor has become is, to put it moderately, not entirely of his own making. On balance, the overriding weight of responsibility lies with parents, teachers and adults; and, by extension, the kind of organisations and institutions they construct to run our affairs. If we wish to understand all that we see in Trevor then we must look to our society – because Trevor is made in Britain.

The problems of how society treats its youth have become increasingly urgent. Yet on television there have been relatively few programmes that confront these issues. When *Made in Britain* was first shown on television, I was surprised when many people asked how such a film could be broadcast. I believe that, given the crisis we now face, a more appropriate question would be: why aren't more films being shown that challenge us to look at what is happening in our society, and to the young in particular? The answer lies in the censorship of television.

Censorship in television

In April 1985 I wrote an article for *The Guardian* that examined how censorship often prevents controversial films from being shown. Shortly afterwards a government minister (Leon Brittan, then Home Secretary) publically intervened to suppress a *Real Lives* programme on Northern Ireland. This was unusual, as most censorship takes place within television companies themselves (although jobs at the BBC are vetted by MI5). Censorship of television is an on-going, everyday process.

The banned television play is a rare beast; but, like the schoolboy send out of the classroom, it is an important indicator of accepted values and levels of tolerance. Though being an author of a banned play makes one a member of an élite club, membership is a very poor substitute to one's work being seen on television. And, as a writer, I have no ambition to join even though the possibility is ever present.

Censorship in British television is a reality. Scripts are written, programmes are produced, and the companies respond: 'It would not be wise to make this. It's unbalanced. I do not think we can show this at this time.' Such statements tend to proliferate in the wake of programmes likely to worry the executives.

Usually it is the play or programme that draws on contemporary issues that is the most likely candidate for the executive boot (although Ken Griffiths's *Collins* – a historian's comments on the great Irish politician – showed that it is possible for a historical subject to tread on a contemporary nerve). It is sometimes said that a programme is kept from our screens because it is poorly executed; although, if this were true, I would have thought there would be more blank screens up and down the country.

Looking back on three very different examples – *Collins*; a controversial film about Borstal, *Scum*, and Loach's four documentary films on the miners' strike, *Questions of Leadership* – it is easy to see that the decision not to broadcast these programmes was a political decision. It had nothing to do with the quality, but everything to do with the content. Political content. The censorship was political.

But this highly visible form of censorship which usually attracts much publicity is only a small slice from a much broader spectrum of censorship. A greater and more effective form of censorship, by far, is self-censorship – the restrictions we, those who make television, place upon ourselves – stopping the idea before it starts. Or, to put it another way, how much the prevailing ethos (the current ideas and opinions of television management) allows for the exploration and generation of ideas.

Recently I have experienced the same conversation with

different people based on two questions: 'Why was your *Tales Out of School* allowed to be shown?' and 'Why is nobody else making similar programmes?'

The answers are simple: they were shown because they were responsibly produced and did not contravene any guideline in the IBA rule book – why should they not be shown? Such programmes are being made but they are in short supply and that is the way it has always been in television. Yet, in the conversations, there remained an assumption that the broadcasting of the films was an exception to some unwritten rule.

Perhaps these people were responding to a hidden message to be found behind boundless streams of statements on the ratings war, the commercialisation of the BBC, 'Giving the people what they want' and so on. This message reads: 'Don't rock the boat. Don't do anything too radical or unusual. Chances cost too much money. Nobody will want to hear what you have to say.'

Most writers have usually done enough research to know that the television companies hold the monopoly on the technology, the means of production and distribution. Anyone on the outside trying to find a way in – and writers are usually on the outside – tends to follow the much vaunted rules of the market place, of supply and demand, and tries to give the companies that which they think the companies want. They follow trends and imitate what they see on TV. Ask any professional script reader. But the sad thing is that 99.5% of all this material is junked. All that wasted effort hits the bin. Writers face great pressure to keep to subjects and ideas that are familiar and conventional.

But there is no monopoly on ideas. Ideas are free. But how free people feel to explore ideas depends on the degree they are encouraged or discouraged to undertake the exploration. It depends on the general cultural and political environment – and on how much television companies are prepared to 'rock the boat'. Most ideas are censored and never reach the screen.

Censorship in television and in schools: are there parallels?

There are powerful parallels between television and schools. Both institutions put the consumer on the passive receiving end of predetermined, selected (censored) sequences of information and messages. Both institutions hold monopolies on the means of production and communication. They determine the content. As individuals, we have little power to change the content or the structure of these institutions – even though we may see how they might effectively be changed.

Yet school is the one place where, as a society, we accept a collective responsibility for what happens to the people within that institution – our children (after that, kids, you're on your own). If we wish to examine why we fail to produce a particular brand of drama on television then we might also take a critical look at our collective responsibilities and ask if our schools are a fertile breeding ground for discussion, criticism and debate?

Television is the most important medium of communication invented since the advent of the telephone, paper, the ballpoint pen and, before that, talking. It is a fact that many people watch television in preference to indulging in any of the latter.

Drama on television, therefore, is important. And the essence of any drama is that it breaks taboos. If it doesn't get its fingers into that which we prefer to ignore, then it's not drama. It has to articulate the unspoken. There are lots of taboos in our society, whole herds of sacred cows, yet I see no positive movement in our schools which encourages a critical perspective on the society in which we live.

To many controlling education, criticism is taboo, judgement by the authority is all. Children have no voice in the eleven years of compulsory education they are required to receive. Their criticisms are not invited. As a recent *Times* editorial stated, 'All education is a battle to capture the minds of the young.'

The attitude of the current Secretary of State for Education towards the spirit of enquiry and the free expression of ideas is worth noting. As recently reported in *The Sunday Times*, in English Keith Joseph urged greater emphasis on the teaching of grammar. Form before content. In Physics, the examination councils have been advised to omit references to 'the social and economic issues which arise from scientific knowledge'. In Chemistry and Biology, taboo subjects include 'pollution control', 'problems of inadequate world feed supply, harmful effects of pesticides and harmful uses of fertilisers and drugs' and 'the beneficial and harmful effects of fossil fuels and alternative energy sources'. The examination system dominates the school curriculum and, therefore, the subjects which are raised and discussed in the classroom.

Speculation on any issue, such as the discussion of the implications of a non-nuclear future, which might be seen as contrary to government policies and dictates, is construed as indoctrination. Yet indoctrination in schools, as on television, is more often a case of what is left out. Why shouldn't pupils debate a non-nuclear future, the value of the education they receive, the treatment of the young in our society, or other controversial issues? Why shouldn't children criticise the education system – and teachers – if there is something wrong? Too often schools become places where children are taught to accept without question the teachers, the curriculum, and the system of education. Add to this the ingredient of teacher assessment, a system of promotional rewards to be judged according to performance . . . a battle for the minds of the young, indeed.

If any child emerges from school life with his or her critical factors intact then it can only be by the (subversive) virtues of the individual teacher and not because it is in any way embodied in the system. Speculation, inquiry and criticism are no more at the heart of the British educational system than at the heart of any other British institution.

Where, in that lot, are we to find tomorrow's innovative

writers and producers? The terms of success are dictated by the system, so many marks out of ten, and from a very early age we are taught to trim our talents to that which we are told will lead to success.

But success is not simply a matter of ability, it is also a matter of selection. As a recent Department of Education and Science internal discussion document states, 'There has to be selection because we are beginning to create aspirations which society cannot match . . . When young people drop off the education production line and cannot find work at all, or work which meets their abilities and expectations, then we are only creating frustration with perhaps disturbing social consequences . . . If we have a highly educated and idle population we may possibly anticipate more serious social conflict. People must be educated once more to know their place.'

Fortunately, on television, in schools, and in society itself, experience and adversity often undo many of these dubious lessons. People become articulate in adversity. Words as well as action – vehement argument and discussion – become essential weapons in the fight to resolve conflict. The experiences of riots in Brixton, life in detention centres, standing on the picket lines, generate fierce discussions. In adversity, people become articulate and critical of themselves, their situation, and the forces with which they find themselves in conflict. From this adversity, they glean a painful sense of the gulf, the ever-widening gap, that exists between their own experiences and the way the media tells their story, or fails to tell their story at all. A painful education.

The backlash becomes inevitable and leaves behind a bitterness and an awareness that *everything* we see on television is political and that there is no such thing as an impartial, balanced point of view.

David Leland
October 1985.

Made in Britain was first transmitted on ITV in Britain on 10 July 1983. Given below are the credits and cast for this Central Independent Television production.

Credits

Production Manager	Guy Travers
1st Assistant Director	Roy Stevens
Location Manager	Joanna Gollins
Continuity	Ene Watts
Production Assistant	Monica Rogers
Assistant Directors	Richard Dobson, Chris Thompson
Camera Assistants	Jeremy Gee, Ian Owles, James Ainslie
Grip	Peter Hall
Gaffer	Ronnie Rampton
Sound Assistants	Tony Bell, Clive Osborne
Dubbing Editor	Kevin Brazier
Assistant Editor	Clive Gardener
Dubbing Mixer	Mike Billing
Make-up	Mary Hillman
Wardrobe	Daryl Bristow
Property Master	Bobby Hedges
Accounts Assistant	Joan Murphy
Assistant Art Director	Celia Barnett
Costumes	Monica Howe
Music by	The Exploited
Production Executive	Sue Wall
Casting Director	Sheila Trezise
Sound Mixer	Tony Jackson
Editor	Steve Singleton
Art Director	Jamie Leonard
Photographed by	Chris Menges
Associate Producer	Patrick Cassavetti
Written by	David Leland
Producer	Margaret Matheson
Directed by	Alan Clarke

Cast

Trevor	Tim Roth
Errol	Terry Richards
Peter Clive	Bill Stewart
Harry Parker	Eric Richard
Superintendent	Geoffrey Hutchings
Barry Giller	Sean Chapman
Policeman	John Bleasdale
Solicitor	Noel Diacomo
Magistrate	Maurice Quick
House Parent	Sharon Courtney
Job Centre Youth	Stephen Sweeney
Job Centre Girls	Kim Benson, Catherine Clarke
Job Centre Woman	Jean Marlow
Chef	Jim Dunk
Canteen Manager	Vass Anderson
Leroy	David Baldwin
Hopkins	Allister Bain
Policeman	Richard Bremmer
Men on Stairs	Brian Hayes, Jiri Stanislav
Viv Parker	Frankie Cosgrove
P.C. Anson	Christopher Fulford

Note on the text: The text which follows differs from the broadcast version of the film in a number of minor ways. A list of changes is given in the appendix.

Made in Britain

Part One

1   Interior. Juvenile Court. Day.   1

The anteroom just outside the juvenile courtroom. Beyond the anteroom there is the main entrance hall which is full of JUVENILE OFFENDERS, SOCIAL WORKERS, SOLICITORS, etc.

In the anteroom: tight close-up on TREVOR's face. He stares straight ahead. Direct. TREVOR is sixteen years old. His hands, arms, body and face are tattooed. He is a skinhead.

TREVOR stands up. His name has been called by the COURT USHER.

As TREVOR gets up, fade in music, hard and loud.

TREVOR walks into the courtroom, very confident. He is followed by a POLICEMAN, a SOLICITOR and his SOCIAL WORKER, HARRY PARKER. PARKER is in his late thirties and speaks with a South London accent.

Camera stays tight on TREVOR as he walks into the courtroom.

2   Interior. Juvenile Court. Day.   2

The POLICEMAN refers to his notebook as he gives his evidence to the MAGISTRATE, COUNCILLOR SAMUEL TOWNSEND, JP.

TREVOR sits, a relaxed and casual observer of the proceedings.

POLICEMAN
Mr Shahnawaz saw Trevor throw a brick through his lounge window. Mr Shahnawaz was treated by his doctor for a cut he received but was later able to identify Trevor when he was apprehended and arrested by the police. Trevor was charged at Rackman Street Police Station at 9:45 p.m. and, asked if he'd anything to say, he made no reply.

MAGISTRATE
Do you have any questions on the facts, Mr Wyman?

SOLICITOR
No questions.

MAGISTRATE
Thank you. Were you aware that Mr Shahnawaz had to be treated for a wound which you inflicted upon him?

TREVOR
Yes.

MAGISTRATE
Stand up.

TREVOR stands up.

MAGISTRATE
You do not invite leniency, do you?

TREVOR
(thinks about it)
No.

Titles and Music (**UK82** – The Exploited)

3   **Interior Juvenile Court. Day.**   **3**

The MAGISTRATE reads through and refers to the file of notes on TREVOR.

MAGISTRATE
You were a constant truant at school, a failure, it
seems. You have been before the Court on
numerous occasions for non-attendance. You have
been convicted of taking and driving away, shoplifting, violent behaviour and, in spite of your
undertakings to the Court, you have made no
attempts to secure yourself a job. And now you
have been accused of stealing once again and you
have attacked a member of the immigrant
community and caused damage to his property.
It's a long, depressing list. Are you not ashamed
of yourself?

TREVOR
No.

---

4   Int. Juvenile Court. Day.   4

Music.

TREVOR leaves the juvenile courtroom, straight through the
anteroom where the next case is waiting to go into the
Magistrate, and on through the main entrance hall where
flocks of JUVENILE OFFENDERS, SOCIAL WORKERS and
SOLICITORS are still waiting.

The POLICEMAN and SOLICITOR peel off the procession until
only HARRY PARKER remains as escort.

TREVOR and PARKER walk down the stairs and out into the
street.

Cut music and into:

---

5   Int./Exterior. Parker's car. Day.   5

Streets with heavy traffic: TREVOR and PARKER travel to
Hooper Street Assessment Centre. They know each other
well. PARKER spells out the facts to TREVOR as they drive
along in the car.   17

PARKER

You have just been promoted in the Juvenile
Offenders League from a supervision order to a
care order. That means you have been placed in
the care of the Social Services. You are currently
under way to the Hooper Street Residential
Assessment Centre. Residential means a place
where you reside/live. You will reside/live at
Hooper Street for a period of 4/6 weeks, which
means you'll probably end up in there for about
six months while a team of experts, psychiatrists
and psychologists, team leaders, key workers,
decide what they think should be done with you.
That is called assessment. Then you go back in
front of his nibs for nicking the cassettes from
Harrods, he reads the experts' reports and then
sentences you to be hanged. You got that?

TREVOR

What did I get for the cassettes?

PARKER

You don't listen, do you? You're all the
same. Today was the brick through the Paki's
window. They made a   , so you've got to
go back for the cassettes from Harrods. That's
when he'll decide what to do with you.

TREVOR

You didn't help much, did you?

PARKER
(rattled)

How many times have you walked out of that
Court with a caution, a supervision order, when
you should have had your   chopped off?
You're lucky you're not off to a DC or borstal.

TREVOR

Full of

PARKER
You end up in a DC you'll get more than

TREVOR
You in a bad mood, Harry?

PARKER
Did you think you'd get away with it?

TREVOR
What?

PARKER
What? – Nicking from Harrods.

TREVOR
Why not?

PARKER
Was it full of skinheads, the day you went, was it?

TREVOR
It was full of wogs.

PARKER
How many other skinheads did you see doing
their weekly shop?

TREVOR
It was full of wogs, why not me?

PARKER
You heard what he said. No more chances. Go
back in front of him, he'll put you away.

TREVOR
    I'll kick the door down.

PARKER
It's not worth it, Trevor. They'll lock you up.

TREVOR
Can't lock me up for not getting a job.

PARKER
No? Try him and see.

TREVOR
You still going to be my social worker, Harry?

PARKER
Yes, I'm afraid so. I'm off for the next two weeks
so behave yourself.

TREVOR
Off what?

PARKER
Work.

TREVOR
You going on holiday, Harry?

PARKER
That's right.

TREVOR
Where?

PARKER
Corfu.

TREVOR
Where's that?

PARKER
Look, just stay straight 'til I get back.

TREVOR
Put me in your filing cabinet, Harry, I can spend
the next two weeks reading all the cobblers you
write about me.

The front entrance hall, an open reception area leading to the front door. Doors lead off from the hall to other parts of the building.

PARKER and TREVOR are waiting for PETER CLIVE, the Deputy Superintendent of the Assessment Centre.

> PARKER
> You'll be alright here, Trev. Loads of pocket money. Be a good boy and they'll take you on trips down the river, horse riding, camping, take you Paki bashing down Southall, if you're lucky.

CLIVE walks through the corridor on his way to his office.

> PARKER
> Peter, this is Trevor.

> CLIVE
> Hello, Trevor. Harry. Yes . . . what can I do for you, Harry?

> PARKER
> I've brought Trevor.

> CLIVE
> You mean this Trevor?

> PARKER
> Yeah, that's right, yeah. His case notes will be round later, in a lorry.

> CLIVE
> Slight confusion here, Harry – have you brought Trevor for admission?

> PARKER
> We've just come from the Court.

> CLIVE
> I know nothing about this.

PARKER
It's a telephone referral.

CLIVE
When?

PARKER
Four or five days ago.

CLIVE
Ah, well, yes. Wait there.

CLIVE goes into the front office to collect the log book.

TREVOR
How did you know I was coming four, five days ago?

PARKER
I didn't.

TREVOR
I only went to Court this morning.

PARKER
It's common procedure.

CLIVE comes out of the front office carrying the log book.

CLIVE
Come through, will you, Harry. Er . . . you too, Trevor. We'll see if we can't sort this out.

PARKER
(to Trevor)
Come on . brain. We'll find you a place even if I have to pay for it.

They follow CLIVE to his office. CLIVE produces a large bunch of keys and unlocks the door. A room that is not occupied is always locked. Keys prevail: office doors, cupboards, drawers, etc. are always locked. CLIVE is in his late thirties. A somewhat harrassed individual, he gives the impression of someone three weeks behind on schedule.

Clive's office. A bit of a mess.

TREVOR sits on the window-sill.

> CLIVE
> Harry, Trevor's a telephone referral, isn't he?

> PARKER
> Right.

The telephone rings. CLIVE answers it and checks the log book.

> CLIVE
> Hello, Peter Clive.
> (to himself)
> Beep beep beep beep . . . Hello, Peter Clive.
> Terry. Yes. She's still here. No, nothing's planned,
> no . . . er, can you hold on two ticks, Terry? Yes.
> Good.

CLIVE puts his hand over the mouthpiece of the telephone.

> CLIVE
> Harry. Your message isn't recorded in the log.
> Terry's not expected.

> PARKER
> Trevor.

> CLIVE
> Trevor. That makes things difficult for us to sort
> out.

> PARKER
> Impossible I'd say, Peter.

> CLIVE
> Yes.

> PARKER
> Don't let it get to you, chum, just remembered I
> left the care order round at the Court.

CLIVE
We can't admit him without a care order.

TREVOR
When can I get down the job centre?

The pips are going on the phone, more money being fed in.

CLIVE
Pardon?

TREVOR
Where is it anyway?

CLIVE
Just a tick.
(back on the phone)
Terry? Can I call you back? Oh. Well then come tomorrow. At eleven. I'll make a note of that. Yes. Bye.

Phone down.

PARKER
(to Trevor, over Clive's telephone conversation)
What's brought this on?

TREVOR
This place is full of   Harry, I'd rather work than be here.

CLIVE
Harry.

PARKER
Look, Peter, can't we do something with Trevor, like send him off to get hanged and then you and me can have a sort out?

CLIVE
Alright, I'll take you through and pass you on to someone else,
(to Trevor)
if you feel OK about that?

PARKER
You don't need me to hold your hand, do you?

TREVOR
I want to get down to the job centre as soon as possible, Harry.

CLIVE looks for his keys.

CLIVE
Right, Trevor, come through will you? Back in two ticks Harry.

PARKER
Watch your step,

TREVOR
Bollocks.

TREVOR and CLIVE, keys in hand, walk along a corridor and through a doorway.

CLIVE
What's this about the job centre, Trevor?

TREVOR
Magistrate's told me to get a   job.

8   Int. Staircase. Day.   8

TREVOR and CLIVE walk up a staircase and along another corridor.

CLIVE
I'm Peter Clive, one of two deputy superintendents. I'll link you up with your key worker or house parent . . . if we can find them. They'll fill up your entrance forms with you, organise a room . . . once we've got things sorted. We've got things going here like bike workshops, if you're interested, evening groups, Red Rover days. Oh, and we'll need to have a little conference with you about your contract.

Room: two single beds.

ERROL, a black youth of fourteen, is lying on his bed.
TREVOR leans against a wall and looks across to ERROL.

> TREVOR
> I don't like that bed, it's too near the window,
> there's a draught. I want that one.

> ERROL
> I'm in this bed.

> TREVOR
> I know you are.

> ERROL
> You got a swastika on your head.

> TREVOR
> I know I have.

> ERROL
> I'll sell it to you.

> TREVOR
> What's all this bollocks about a contract?

> ERROL
> Peter Clive, he makes you do it. They make you
> sign a contract.

> TREVOR
> He's a wanker.

> ERROL
> He's a prick. You have to promise to behave and
> get to school on time, that sort of thing. Do it in
> your own writing, write it out and sign it.

> TREVOR
> What school?

ERROL

I still go to my proper school. I been suspended
but I'm back.

TREVOR

So why ain't you there today?

ERROL

I got an infection in my ear. My case conference
comes up next week.

TREVOR takes one half of a smallish pair of scissors from his
pocket. The point has been sawn off.

ERROL

Then I might get out of here.

TREVOR

They're all wankers.

ERROL

Who?

TREVOR

This lot here.

ERROL

What's that?
        (the scissors)

TREVOR

Don't you know?

ERROL

No . . . Here, you can have this bed if you want.

TREVOR

No, thanks. I'll stay over here.

TREVOR flops onto his bed and lies down.

Friday morning.

TREVOR has been given cash for a bus fare by JACKIE
MILTON, a house parent. He follows her down a staircase to
her office.

> TREVOR
> That's just for the bus.

> MILTON
> That's right.

> TREVOR
> What about pocket money?

> MILTON
> You've only just got here, it's not been fixed yet. I
> don't know how much you're supposed to get.

> TREVOR
> The same as everybody else.

> MILTON
> You have damages to pay, don't you, for the
> broken window?

> TREVOR
> I need some pocket money.

> MILTON
> What for? If you're just going down to the job
> centre and back, you won't need any pocket
> money. You go straight there and back again.

> TREVOR
> What if I don't make it back here for lunch?

> MILTON
> It won't take that long. If it was up to me, you
> wouldn't be going at all.

> TREVOR
> They might send me for a job.

MILTON gives in and takes a pound note from the cash tin.

>MILTON
>Here's an extra pound against your pocket money.

TREVOR takes the pound and leaves.

11   Ext. Side street. Day.   11

ERROL leans against a wall, waiting. TREVOR emerges from a shop round the corner. He is opening a new packet of cigarettes; cellophane and silver paper make instant litter. ERROL links up as TREVOR passes and they walk off down the street.

>ERROL
>Where we going?

No reply from TREVOR. He is doing a visual check-out on the cars parked in the street. He settles for a beat-up Morris Minor. He gives the door a few upward tugs and it opens. He opens the passenger door and ERROL gets in.

12   Int. Morris Minor. Day.   12

This is a learning experience for ERROL. TREVOR takes the half-scissors from his pocket.

>TREVOR
>Remember this?

TREVOR forces the half-scissors into the ignition. He then twists and turns it until the ignition makes contact. He starts the engine.

They drive off in the car.

13   Ext. Street. Day.   13

The Morris Minor is parked outside a hardware store. TREVOR walks out of the store and throws a tin in the air and catches it.

A quiet side street. Inside the car: TREVOR takes a small, clear plastic bag from his pocket and unfolds it. He pours the contents of the tin into the plastic bag.

>TREVOR
>Evo Stik –

TREVOR puts the bag into his mouth, blows into it and breathes in the contents, then passes it to ERROL. ERROL blows into the bag and breathes in. This is his initiation into glue sniffing.

>TREVOR
>Stay here.

TREVOR opens the car door and gets out.

>ERROL
>I feel sick.

The job centre is a corner building situated on a busy high street and a quiet side street.

Inside the job centre: boards display jobs available, job centre EMPLOYEES at desks, various PEOPLE waiting for interviews and looking at the job display boards.

Most jobs are typed on small cards and slotted into display boards, some of the choice jobs are written up in pentel on large cards. One of these takes TREVOR's attention: 'Man/ Woman. HGV III driver. 25 +. Local deliveries. Clean licence. £100 p.w. *plus*.'

There is a large notice written which says: 'Youth Opportunities Programme. It's going to work. Ask at reception.'

TREVOR scans the YOP job cards. He emanates the smell of
Evo Stick.

Among the people looking at the cards, there is a YOUTH
who cannot read.

>YOUTH
>(to Trevor)
Oi, what's this say?

>TREVOR
>(reads)
'Supermarket. 23.55 per week.'
That's . . . 50p an hour. Bollocks!

>YOUTH
Yeah.

TREVOR moves to the Youth Employment Board. The YOUTH
follows him.

Unseen, on the other side of the display board, there are two
women, SALLY and JOANNE (20s), reading some of the
cards.

Followed by the YOUTH, TREVOR starts to collect various
cards from the boards.

>YOUTH
You ain't supposed to take the cards.
>(smells the glue)
You a carpenter?

>SALLY
>(out of view)
What about this one, Jo?

>JOANNE (OOV)
I was looking at this one. 'Dental practice.
4 O-levels required to train for 3 years as dental
nurse. Should have knowledge of French and
Spanish, but not essential.'

SALLY (OOV)
Yeah, who'd you have to suck off to get that one then?

JOANNE (OOV)
Right.

YOUTH
(to Trevor)
Here you are, what's this one say?

TREVOR
(reads)
'M/F, 9.30 5.30. Young person for general warehouse duties – must be able to speak fluent Punjabi and Urdu.' You speak Urdu?

YOUTH
No.

TREVOR
(takes the card)
Fucks your chances then, don't it?

TREVOR takes another card.

TREVOR
Here you are.
(reads)
'Wood veneer wall coverings. Candidate must read, be of good character, living at home with parents in home environment. No criminal record. School records will be checked.'

TREVOR stuffs the card into the YOUTH's T-shirt and holding his bundle of cards walks over to one of the reception desks. The WOMAN is interviewing a CLIENT.

TREVOR
Do I get a job from you?

WOMAN
Yes, but you'll have to wait, dear. There's a queue.

TREVOR
You get me a job, right?

WOMAN
Yes, but you can't jump the queue – and you're supposed not to take the cards from the display. Do you think you could put them back for me?

TREVOR
Tacky jobs, ain't they?

WOMAN
If you wait perhaps we can sort something out.

TREVOR
Have you got something useful I can do while I'm waiting for a job? I got ten O-levels, seven A-levels, I speak fluent Punjabi and Chapatti.

WOMAN
You'll have to wait.

TREVOR
I'll come back tomorrow.

He throws the job cards onto the desk and leaves the job centre.

YOUTH
See you.

TREVOR
I doubt it.

16   Ext. Job centre. Day.   16

TREVOR walks out of the job centre. He stands motionless for a few seconds staring at the job centre window. He picks up a large concrete block from a pile of builder's rubble and throws it at the window. The large expanse of plate glass shatters onto the pavement. TREVOR walks off down the side street.

17	**Int. Derelict building. Day.**	17

A burst of sunlight as TREVOR smashes open the front door into the derelict building. As the door smacks against the wall, the sound echoes through the building. TREVOR strides along the corridor followed by ERROL.

> ERROL
> What's this place?

TREVOR pushes open a double-door into:

18	**Int. Swimming pool. Day.**	18

A derelict swimming pool. No water in the pool. Chairs, empty boxes, general litter scatters the area. Along the right-hand side of the pool are empty changing cubicles.

TREVOR jumps into the empty pool. ERROL follows. They walk to one corner and TREVOR reaches into a water inlet opening in the wall and pulls out a bundle wrapped in cloth.

TREVOR unwraps the bundle to reveal a large bunch of car keys, a hammerhead, a centre punch and a T-bar.

> ERROL
> Hey, where'd you get all them?

There are at least a hundred keys.

> TREVOR
> Down the scrap yard.

> ERROL
> (pointing to the centre punch)
> What's this?

> TREVOR
> Centre punch. Automatic. You never seen one?

> ERROL
> No.

TREVOR shows ERROL the T-bar.

> TREVOR
> T-bar.

> ERROL
> Whassat for?

> TREVOR
> I'll show you.
> (he gives Errol the keys)
> Take these. Get them in the Centre, hide them,
> stick 'em up your arse, don't lose them. We get
> nicked, chuck 'em.

TREVOR pockets the hammerhead, centre punch and T-bar
and stuffs the empty bundle back into the hole. They climb
out of the pool and leave.

19   Ext. Street. Day.   19

A street full of parked cars. TREVOR and ERROL walk down
the street.

> ERROL
> All the new cars, they got locks, proper locks.
> How you gonna do it if you ain't got the right size
> keys?

> TREVOR
> Which one you want?

ERROL picks a new Ford Granada.

> ERROL
> That one.

TREVOR takes the automatic centre punch from his pocket,
places it against the car window, presses the button and the
window disintegrates. He is into the car in seconds. He
unlocks the rear door and ERROL climbs into the back seat.

ERROL
See, it's locked.

TREVOR
Bollocks!

ERROL
You want the keys?

TREVOR
No.

TREVOR takes the T-bar and hammerhead from his pocket. Places the end of the T-bar into the ignition keyhole and strikes the other end with the hammerhead. He hits it several times, forcing the T-bar into the ignition system, breaking the internal mechanism in the process. He then twists and turns the T-bar until the ignition makes contact. The engine turns and roars into life.

ERROL
Oh that's sweet, man, that's sweet.

TREVOR
Now get out.

ERROL
What?

TREVOR
Get out.

ERROL
What for?

TREVOR
I've been to the job centre, right, on the bus. We get back at the same time, they'll sus and then they'll get my keys, so you fuckin walk. I'm going to see some mates.

ERROL is deeply disappointed. He gets out of the car.

TREVOR drives off in the Ford Granada.

The forecourt of Hooper Street Assessment Centre.

TREVOR has parked the Ford Granada and is smoking a cigarette while finishing off the remains of a Macburger. PETER CLIVE rides past on his Honda 99cc and sees TREVOR getting out of the car.

CLIVE heads off TREVOR as he walks towards the main entrance of the Assessment Centre.

> CLIVE
> Trevor.

No response. TREVOR walks on.

> CLIVE
> Trevor!

TREVOR stops.

> CLIVE
> Take it back.

> TREVOR
> What?

> CLIVE
> The car, Trevor. Take it back!

> TREVOR
> I don't know what you're talking about.

> CLIVE
> I'm not bloody stupid. I saw you. You've nicked that bloody car, so take it back.

> TREVOR
> I ain't nicked no car.

> CLIVE
> I saw you get out of it, now I'm not blind or stupid – now take it back. Get rid of it!

TREVOR
I'll get rid of it, but I ain't taking it back.

CLIVE
Fine. Do just that.

TREVOR walks off towards the Ford Granada.

21   Int. Lavatory at Hooper Street. Day.   21

ERROL in the lavatory. He removes the lid from the cistern, drops the keys into the cistern, and then replaces the lid.

He takes out the carefully folded polythene glue bag from his pocket and takes a good snort.

22   Int. Hooper Street. Day.   22

The Entrance Hall: there are large plastic bags, hold-alls and cardboard boxes full of food.

JACKIE MILTON and BARRY GILLER (house parents) are in a confrontation with a group of GIRLS. The argument is about a trip down the river which has been organised, but now some of the girls have decided to back out.

PETER CLIVE is in his office. During the argument, TREVOR comes in by the front doorway and is waylaid by CLIVE.

A disjointed muddled argument.

MILTON
You've known about it for two weeks.

SHARON
I haven't known till now.

TINA
I been on a boat before.

GILLER
Let's get some stuff loaded. Come on.

MILTON
Won't you at least come and have a look at it?

SHARON
Look, what do I want to look at a bleedin boat for?

TINA
I've been on a hovercraft so I ain't scared of a
barge, am I?

SHARON
I know you ain't.

TINA
He said I was, he said I was bloody scared.

GILLER
I did not. I said if you were nervous you should
come down and have a look, that's all.

TINA
I don't want to.

CLIVE
Trevor, come through will you?

MILTON
It's two – three days –

GILLER
We go down as far as Send and then back again.

SHARON
Go, and bloody good luck.

The above conversation recedes as TREVOR makes his way to
CLIVE's office.

| 23 | **Int. Clive's office. Day.** | **23** |

CLIVE
Where is it? Where did you put it?

TREVOR
What?

CLIVE
The bloody car, Trevor, the car.

TREVOR
I gave it to Oxfam – they're using it to ship Wogs back to Zulu land.

CLIVE
Where is it?

TREVOR
Police parking lot, Broadway Lane. Where's lunch?

CLIVE
Why did you take it?

TREVOR
To get back to lunch.

CLIVE
You were given money for a bus.

TREVOR
I bought a car instead.

CLIVE
You're not being clever, you know.

TREVOR
When do I get lunch?

CLIVE
You don't. You've missed lunch. It's too late.

TREVOR
You what?

CLIVE
Next time I'll have you down that courtroom so fast you won't know what happened.

TREVOR
Great.

CLIVE
It's your last chance. Get out.

TREVOR kicks the filing cabinet and leaves the office.

24   **Int. Canteen. Day.**   24

The canteen is empty except for ERROL who sits at one of the tables, somewhat glued out of his brain. TREVOR comes in from the direction of the entrance hall.

TREVOR
You had your lunch?

ERROL
Yeah.

TREVOR
I ain't.

TREVOR goes over to the canteen service counter. The CHEF, a big man, is eating his lunch whilst reading the newspaper.

TREVOR
Oi! Oi! I want my lunch!

The CHEF walks over to the service hatch and rolls down the blind without saying a word.

The canteen manager, PEARSON, appears from his small office on the other side of the open area.

PEARSON
Do you mind? There's no lunch. You know there's no lunch. We don't serve lunch at three in the afternoon.

TREVOR
He's got his in there, he's got it.

> PEARSON
> The dining-room's closed.

PEARSON goes back into his office. TREVOR sits down next to ERROL. Passive. Still. Then he gets up and takes a flying leap at the canteen manager's door. It smacks open. Then a flying leap at the kitchen door. It shakes under his attack. Another flying leap. And another.

The CHEF comes out via the other door.

> CHEF
> Bastard! I'll have you!

TREVOR's boot connects with the CHEF's crutch. As might be expected, the CHEF falls to the ground. TREVOR puts in the boot a couple more times before GILLER hits him with a flying tackle pinning him to the wall.

25   Int. Corridor at Hooper Street. Day.   25

The door at the end of the corridor explodes open. The CHEF has got TREVOR round the neck and one arm twisted into a lock. TREVOR fights for his life as he is forced along the corridor. GILLER grabs one of TREVOR's arms as CLIVE picks his way past the group to unlock a door.

> CLIVE
> Let me through, I have the keys, I've got to get through. OK.

CLIVE unlocks the door then gets well out of the way as the CHEF and GILLER thrust TREVOR into a large, empty basement room.

> GILLER
> Alright.

The door is locked. We see TREVOR through the glass panel in the door. He stands, legs apart, and takes in his surroundings. He starts to pace forcefully round the room, smiling, as if he has achieved a victory.

Part Two

A long, empty room. It used to be a classroom but is now
used on a casual basis as 'The Quiet Room'. A space where
troublemakers can be left to cool out. Fluorescent tube
lighting, no furniture, a blackboard which is fixed across one
wall at the end of the room.

'Wankers' is written across the blackboard in white chalk.
TREVOR is sitting on the floor with his head resting against
the wall.

Sound of keys in the door: enter GORDON HOUSE,
superintendent of the assessment centre, BARRY GILLER and
PETER CLIVE. TREVOR doesn't move. HOUSE takes in
TREVOR while still on the move. GILLER and CLIVE stick to
the perimeter of the room.

HOUSE registers 'Wankers' written on the blackboard.

> HOUSE
> Get rid of this, shall we?

He looks round for the board rubber.

> TREVOR
> (to Giller and Clive)
> Heavy mob?

> CLIVE
> Here.

CLIVE gives the board rubber to HOUSE.

> HOUSE
> Thank you, Peter.

HOUSE rubs the word 'Wankers' from the board.

HOUSE

At least you can spell. Harry Parker, your social
worker – I know Harry very well – he says you're
bright, says you're worth a bit of bother.

TREVOR

I wouldn't take the time if I were you.

HOUSE

Don't be clever, don't be smart. We've no time to
waste, get that. Plenty of other kids we could be
dealing with. If you really want to behave like a
moron we'll put you with all the other morons –
under lock and key at Hatchmere House. And I
can do that, I'll have you transferred to a secure
unit, we'll do your assessment from there. If
you're going to stay here, let's make it clear,
you're going to have to step into line, just a sec,
you're going to have to step into line and you're
going to have to co-operate. Now, that shouldn't
be too difficult – we're a reasonable lot.

TREVOR

I'm not signing any contract.

HOUSE

Well, let's look at that, shall we? Let's give your
intelligence the benefit of the doubt. Mr Parker
says you're a bright lad and I respect his opinion.
So I have a particular interest in you. Personal
between the two of us. I want you to prove to me
you're worth all the time and effort that we're
prepared to put into you. Your big break this,
because I'll not give you a second chance. Alright?

TREVOR

Alright.

TREVOR stands up.

HOUSE
Good. So let's take a look at what life's got in store
for you, go back a few steps, see just how clever
you've been so far.

He sets off at a good pace and keeps it up.

HOUSE
For a kick-off, you've just been to Court haven't
you? When was it?

HOUSE writes out 'COURT' on the blackboard. Throughout
the following dialogue he writes the key words on the
blackboard. The blackboard finally reads:

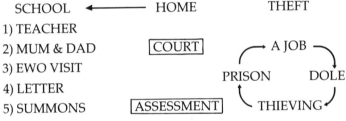

SCHOOL ⟵———— HOME   THEFT
1) TEACHER
2) MUM & DAD   COURT   → A JOB
3) EWO VISIT   PRISON   DOLE
4) LETTER
5) SUMMONS   ASSESSMENT   THIEVING
6) TEST ATTENDANCE

CLIVE
Thursday, yesterday.

HOUSE
Just yesterday. But you've been to Court before,
haven't you? Right?

TREVOR
Right.

HOUSE
Still being clever, still being smart. So, what were
the most important things that happened to you
before you went to Court, eh? Can you remember
that far back, eh? You started off here – at home.

He writes 'HOME'.

> HOUSE
> H-O-M-E spells home. There's your mum, dad, all
> the rest of them, and just like any other mum and
> dad, all they ask you to do, all you have to do, is
> go to school.

He draws an arrow from 'HOME' to the left-hand side of the
blackboard where he writes 'SCHOOL'.

> HOUSE
> Now that's not much to ask, is it? You're clever,
> bright, everybody wants you to succeed, nobody
> wants a failure on their hands, get the right
> qualifications, make your way in the world. But
> you didn't want to go to school did you? You
> knew best, so you started bunking off. Out the
> gate, over the fence, and your teachers are
> concerned 'cause they're there to help, they don't
> want to see you get behind. So they go to see your
> mum and dad.

He has written '1) TEACHER 2) MUM & DAD'

> TREVOR
> Teacher's never been to my house.

> HOUSE
> No matter. They talked to your mum and dad,
> didn't they? And they told you to get your arse
> back into school. They know you have to go but
> you still didn't listen – out the gate, over the fence,
> and before you know where you are, your mum
> and dad get a visit from the Education Welfare
> Officer. You got a visit from him, didn't you?

He writes '3) EWO VISIT'.

> TREVOR
> Yeah.

HOUSE

That's right – because the EWO's there to make
sure you go to school and if you don't he gives the
nod to the appropriate authority and that spells
trouble. Now, at this point a lot of kids get a bit of
sense. They get themselves together, they get back
to school – they listen. But you didn't listen, did
you? The Education Welfare Officer visits four,
five, six, even seven times, tries to help, discover
the problem, a lot of time and expense and all
because you don't want to go to school.

He writes '4) LETTER' and '5) SUMMONS' in quick
succession.

HOUSE

The EWO reaches his limit, so he sends your
parents a letter threatening to take you to Court
for non-attendance, but that does nothing,
absolutely nothing, so there's a summons and you
go, for the very first time, to Court. Your debut.

He draws a square round the word 'COURT'.

HOUSE

First appearance – send him home for a test
attendance, for whatever good that'll do.

He writes '6) TEST ATTENDANCE'.

HOUSE

You're supposed to go to school for twenty-one
days straight, but you foul up after the third or
fourth day. And back you go again.

He taps the word 'COURT'. He counts down the list.

HOUSE

So, one, two, three, four, five, six breaks. Six
chances to get yourself straight and get your arse
back into school. And one, two, three, four, five,
six times you've blown it – now am I not right?

TREVOR
Yeah.

HOUSE
But you weren't just bunking off were you? You
had to do something with all that free time, so you
did a bit of thieving.

He writes 'THEFT'.

HOUSE
The first two or three times you get caught, you
get taken down the nick and some policeman tells
you off, shouts at you. Next time you get a
caution. This time a sergeant in full uniform
shouts at you, but it doesn't make a damn bit of
difference because you are apparently deaf to any
kind of reason and you go on nicking and making
a general bloody nuisance of yourself when you
should be here!
         (he bangs the word 'SCHOOL' several times)
Learning something useful! But it's burglary,
shoplifting, t.d.a. – touching the dog's arse –
taking and driving away. And back you go to
Court. They're getting to know you now, so you
get fined or sent to the local Police Attendance
Centre, kept off the streets all day Saturday, made
to scrub floors by another loud policeman when
you could be watching West Ham lose at home.
The magistrates don't know what to do with you,
they're all greengrocers and shopkeepers, so they
send you here, to us, for assessment.

He writes 'ASSESSMENT', puts a box round it, and puts
down the chalk.

Hands in pockets, HOUSE strolls up and down the length of
the empty room.

HOUSE

So what are we going to do with you? We could
recommend you go home –

TREVOR

What home?

HOUSE

– but they won't have you. So how are we going to
get rid of you? Foster parents – never. Children's
home – a joke. CHE, Detention Centre, borstal.
Well . . . a pity about the CHE, Community
Home with Education. Appealing both to your
intellectual brilliance and your public spirit. What
used to be called an approved school, a CHE. You
could have been king of the Mafia, lots of 'lick my
arse' power trips for ambitious young fifteen year
olds and you've just turned sixteen. Bad luck. Not
much left to bring you in line, is there? A short,
sharp, shock at the local Detention Centre or
borstal. Two simple lessons you're going to have
to learn, DC or borstal – one: discipline, two:
respect for authority. And you're going to have to
learn it so you might as well learn it now. This is
an open invitation to you to co-operate, Trevor, for
your own good. DC's. Seven out of ten coming
out of detention centres, eight out of ten leaving
borstals re-offend, commit crimes that is, within
two years. So, here you are, fresh out of borstal.
What's the first thing you're going to need – Peter?

CLIVE

A job.

HOUSE writes 'A JOB'.

HOUSE

A job. Peter, how many unemployed do we have
at the moment?

TREVOR

Millions.

HOUSE

Exactly. So what chance have you got with your spots and your record of getting a job against a lad with O and A-levels and a decent haircut?

TREVOR

'Bout nil.

HOUSE

Optimistic – so, no job. What do you do? Sign on. The dole.

He writes 'DOLE'.

HOUSE

How much is that worth to you? A place to live, food in your gut, a bit of fun – nothing, it's gone. Broke. No job, no prospects, no cash, so what do you do?

He writes 'THIEVING'.

HOUSE

And you're back here!

He bangs the word 'COURT' with his finger.

HOUSE

And all because you were too damn stupid when you were here –

He underlines the word 'SCHOOL' several times.

HOUSE

– nicking sweets from the local tuck shop! They've tried all this. They know all this doesn't work. Not with you. So what's left?

He writes 'PRISON'

HOUSE

And you're on the bandwagon, boy, and you won't get off.

He makes a circle by linking each word with an arrow.

> HOUSE
> Prison – locked up like an animal. A job – no
> prospects. Dole – no cash. Thieving – no more
> chances. Prison – an animal. Round and round
> you go. Well, those are your options. You've
> created them. You've brought it all upon yourself.

He chucks down the chalk, dusts off his hands, pleased with
his performance.

> HOUSE
> Before you kick another door down, before you
> kick another chef in the bollocks, before you do
> anything – think. You may not get another chance.
> Settle down, we'll have another little chat on
> Monday.

HOUSE leaves the room, closing the door behind him.
Silence.

> TREVOR
> Sounds great – when do I start?

GILLER and CLIVE are now left with the more practical task of
getting TREVOR out of the room. TREVOR is quite prepared to
sit it out, turning his disadvantage into strength.

> CLIVE
> It doesn't have to be like that, Trevor, there are
> alternatives. There are brighter prospects.

> TREVOR
> You lot are all the same. It's all first names with
> you – 'how do you feel about that Trevor?' You
> make out like you know me.

> CLIVE
> I know some things about you, Trevor –

> TREVOR
> Trevor!

CLIVE
I know you're intelligent, it's all in your reports, you could do well –

TREVOR
You say that like you're giving me a present.

CLIVE
I'm not trying to be patronising, if that's what you mean.

TREVOR
Look, what do you expect me to be? Thick in the head – the way you want me?

GILLER
Trevor –

TREVOR
Trevor!

GILLER
You found your tongue now the superintendent has gone?

TREVOR
Bollocks!

GILLER
You can walk out of this room now –

TREVOR
Where to?

GILLER
But you must behave responsibly.

TREVOR
Grow up?

GILLER
No more violence, right? And start using some of the intelligence you're supposed to have.

CLIVE
That's right.

TREVOR
Bollocks! Piss off! I hate you, the fuckin pair of
you. I hate you!

GILLER
I don't really know you, Trevor, and you don't
know me. So how can you hate me?

TREVOR
For putting me in here.

GILLER
You put yourself in here.

CLIVE
Trevor, look, sorry, you go kicking doors down,
breaking the place up –

TREVOR
I'm British.

GILLER
So?

TREVOR
Do you know what that means, do you?

GILLER
I think so, yes.

TREVOR
Are you proud to be British? Are you?

GILLER
What do you mean, Trevor?

TREVOR
Don't you know? I'm proud.

GILLER
I don't really think about it like that, Trevor.

TREVOR

That's because you spend too much time locked
up in here. With all these niggers.

GILLER

Oh, I see . . . British bulldog, one, two, three.

TREVOR

I'm more British than you are, fuck face. You hate
the blacks as much as I do only you don't admit it.
You hate the blacks more than I do because they
frighten you. That's why you lock them up.

GILLER

Watch your tongue.

TREVOR

You lock up anything that frightens you.

GILLER

The only thing that frightens me, Trevor, are the
people who put sick ideas like that into children's
heads.

CLIVE

Trevor, you are not in prison. This is not a prison.

TREVOR

In here it's just the same as school. Do what we
tell you. Think what we tell you. Say what we tell
you. Squawk. Be a fuckin parrot. I hate you for
putting me in here. You're bullshitters. You
swallow your own bollocks, you expect me to
swallow it too. The blacks in here are thick as shit
with no brains, you know it, admit it. Be honest. I
had to sit in school and watch these wankers
trying to add up on their fingers. I was held back.
All the white kids were held back –

GILLER

Ah, I see – and that is why you spend your time
attacking canteen managers – it's all the fault of
the blacks?

TREVOR
The Pakis don't even speak fuckin English.

GILLER
Send them back.

CLIVE
Now, look, come on –

TREVOR
There's nothing cruel in that, it would be kind.

GILLER
Is that why you threw a brick through Mr
whatever-his-name-is window?

TREVOR
Every Paki's going to get a brick through his
windows, then shit and piss and petrol. Wait 'til it
starts.

GILLER
You're proud of all this, are you?

TREVOR
If I spend my life watching my P's and Q's because
some mingy little fucker like you is going to write
it all down on a bit of paper. 'Your case conference
is coming up, watch your step.' Bollocks! I say
what I want to say, you got decisions to make
about my life, you get on with it, it's got bugger all
to do with me. I hate you for putting me in here.
One day you'll fuckin pay for it.

CLIVE
Trevor, we didn't put you in here. You did that.
You put yourself in here. We're trying to get you
out.

TREVOR
Out where?

CLIVE

Out of this room, out of this place – back into the world!

TREVOR

It's your fuckin world, mate, not mine. You stick it up your arse, I don't want it.

GILLER

Come on, Peter, let's go and have a drink.

TREVOR

What's the matter, can't you take a bit of honesty?

GILLER

Well now, I wouldn't have said that honesty was one of your finer points.

CLIVE

Just a minute, can I just say something, Trevor? Just a minute, that's all. Let's just cool it, shall we? This is a bad start, but there's no need for it to go on like this. No reason at all. What you have to remember is this is just a temporary situation. You could be out of here in no time. You are here for assessment, that's all, and what that means is that we would like to help you to help yourself. Now, it needn't be like that –

(pointing to the blackboard)

there are alternatives. If it goes well, you could be out of here in three or four weeks – there are youth projects, you could travel, apprentice boarding schools, choose a trade, you can still study, loads of things, it needn't be like that. While you're here, there's pocket money, if you want new clothes you can have new clothes. There's trips planned – Christ, it's not as bad as you make it sound. But there has to be some kind of understanding between us –

TREVOR
(to Giller)
What you looking at your watch, for?

GILLER
I wasn't looking at my watch.

TREVOR
What were you doing? Counting the hairs on your arms?

CLIVE
There's a hell of a lot you can enjoy, Trevor, horse riding, motorbike scrambling, canoeing – a lot better than sitting in this bloody room.

TREVOR
What about fucking?

GILLER
Yes, we do have a man who comes round every Thursday to fuck some sense into selected individuals.

TREVOR
You on that one, are you?

CLIVE
The two of you, please! Trevor, let's just concentrate on getting out of here, getting out of this room. We can sort out the world tomorrow.

TREVOR
I'm not signing any contract.

CLIVE
Then forget about the contract, forget about it. All it means is cooperation, and that's what's important. We must cooperate because I tell you, if we don't sort out something, and soon, all that, all that bloody awful mess up there will be the only options left. There will be no more help from us.

TREVOR
Great.

CLIVE
You'll be a total bloody failure – at sixteen – and it's such a bloody waste!

TREVOR
I'm a success, mate, I'm a fuckin star.

GILLER
Then why are you in here, Trevor? There are those among us who would like to know the answer to that. And from where I'm standing it's not looking good.

TREVOR
I'm in exactly the right place at the right time. The fact that you're too fuckin thick or stupid to see that, that marks you down. You'll be put up against a bus, covered in petrol and shot.

GILLER
Fantastic.

TREVOR
All of you. It's you that's fuckin failed. I'm not your bleedin problem or anyone's bleedin problem. Bollocks to you and your report, write it, lock me up. Who gives a fuck?

CLIVE
I don't know, Trevor, I really don't know.
(to Giller)
What are we going to do?

TREVOR
About what?

CLIVE
About you, Trevor.

TREVOR
(very fierce)
No! About you! What the fuck are we going to do about you?!

CLIVE walks away, sighs, looks at his watch.

CLIVE
Shit!

TREVOR
If you had any balls you'd stick a knife in the bastards who write all that bollocks. They're wankers. They're just like the teachers at school. They're all fuckin wankers.

GILLER
You learn anything at school, did you?

TREVOR
Yeah, be the best, otherwise forget it.

GILLER
That it?

TREVOR
Everything they teach you at school is useless.

GILLER
Everything?

TREVOR
It's rubbish in your head, bugger all to do with me and my life.

GILLER
That's what you learned at school?

TREVOR
Work hard, do well, get a job, otherwise you're no good, you're a vandal. That's what I learned. It's a lot of bollocks! Lies! We're all fuckin great, you ain't taking bugger all from us. We hate you. You

TREVOR (cont.)

can lock me in here but you can't take away the hate inside my head. I can still hate you in my head. Don't like that, do you? You can't take a bit of truth, can you?

GILLER

Oh, I don't think you're particularly truthful. Or honest. No, you'd lie with the best of them. You go out thieving, that's not particularly honest. Perhaps school would be a better place if people like you were more honest, set an example.

TREVOR

You really believe all that not nicking from school, not nicking from the local Paki sweet shop bit, don't you? That's being honest, innit?

GILLER

Yes, it is.

TREVOR

You don't really want me to be honest, do you?

GILLER

Yes, I do.

TREVOR

Well, then honestly speaking, I don't think I can honestly keep the peace while I'm incarcerated in this shithouse or any other shithouse, contract or no contract, so there's no point in saying that I will, is there? How's that for honesty?

CLIVE

Yes, but where's it getting us, Trevor?

GILLER

It's not getting us out of this bloody room.

TREVOR

You see, you can't take it, can you? It's the same
when I was at school. I said when I was bored,
when I didn't want to do a lesson, when I wanted
a fag, when I wanted to tell the teacher to fuck off
for being a wanker or kick him in the teeth – but
they couldn't take it. They didn't want me to be
honest in that way. That's why you don't have
lessons in honesty – nine till ten-thirty, honesty –
because they don't want kids to say what they're
really thinking and feeling inside their heads. If
they had lessons like that they'd lose control. They
wouldn't be able to smack you round the head
when they feel like it. You just want me to be
honest when you take me down the nick, it's a fair
cop, guv, or when I fill out a form. Be honest,
don't cheat, don't carry a knife, bend over, let me
search you, make notes about you, keep files on
you. If I'm honest I got nothing to worry about,
have I? You're protecting me from the dishonest
buggers, aren't you? But I can't look at the files,
what's read out by the magistrate, what those
fuckers said about me at school, what's on the
police computer! It's all a lot of bollocks. We're not
talking about honesty, we're talking about sticking
to the rules. All those honest people out there are
just sticking to the rules, but they lie and they
fuckin cheat all the way. They just think they're
being honest because they've swallowed the
bollocks they've been handed. They've been
conned. But I've not been conned. That's why you
can stick your hairy contract up your hairy arse.
It's a dishonest con. If you want to put me in line
well do it! Don't fuckin lie about it. Kick me in the
bollocks if that's what you feel like doing, because
I'll do the same to you when I feel like it. So
goodnight and fuck off to you.

                    GILLER
Well, goodnight to you too. That's it, Peter. I'm
going.

                    CLIVE
Yes . . . just . . .

CLIVE follows GILLER out of the room. They close the door
and stand in the corridor.

                    CLIVE
. . . Just a minute, Barry.

                    GILLER
Forget it. He's a sod. He's psychotic. Have him
transferred to a secure unit. Let someone else deal
with it.

                    CLIVE
Harry Parker. He dropped this one on us. So let's
chuck it back to him.

                    GILLER
He's said he has no intention of keeping the
peace, let's have him locked up.

                    CLIVE
Give Parker a call.

                    GILLER
Do you really think it's worth it?

TREVOR's face suddenly appears at the glass panel in the
door, like a goldfish in a bowl.

CLIVE takes out his large bunch of keys.

                    CLIVE
Here, this one's to my office and this small one's
to the top drawer in my desk, and in there you'll
find my address book. Parker – under 'P'.

GILLER takes the keys and goes.

GILLER
It's a waste of time.

CLIVE
Yes.

CLIVE goes back into the room. He makes no attempt to
guard or secure the door. He hooks it back, leaving it wide
open.

CLIVE
Do you want to go to the toilet?

TREVOR
No, I'll piss on the wall.

CLIVE
We're going to have to send you to Hatchmere
House, you know. Secure unit. Under lock and
key.

TREVOR
Great.

CLIVE
Is that what you want?

TREVOR
It's where I'm going anyway.

CLIVE
Anything you care about?

TREVOR
If I told you you'd confiscate it.

CLIVE is fed up. He looks at his watch and sighs.

CLIVE
Same every night. Late tomorrow. No-one cares
about your little protest, Trevor. No-one gives a
damn. It's totally insignificant. Just you and this
horrible room.

TREVOR thinks about this – perhaps he has exploited this situation for all that it is worth.

>TREVOR
>Yeah . . . right.

>CLIVE
>Barry Giller and I may not be much, but we're all there is. No-one else gives a sod. I'm going banger racing tomorrow night, why not drag yourself along? You're into cars. Take the Social Services for all they've got, eh? Better than sitting around in this hole.

>TREVOR
>Who wants to watch a bunch of wankers smashing up cars?

>CLIVE
>Oh me, for one. I quite enjoy it. We've got one of our lads entered. It's part of a project. Leroy, he's . . . he's a good driver.

>TREVOR
>And a nigger. I'll go if I can drive.

>CLIVE
>Yes, well, a cut above cruising in a Ford Granada.

>TREVOR
>Accessory. I'll go if I can drive.

>CLIVE
>Keep the peace?

>TREVOR
>If I can drive.

>CLIVE
>It's not that easy, it takes weeks . . . just a minute, just a minute . . . think, think . . .

            (to himself)
if I can get him to . . . yes . . . why not? It's
possible.
            (brightens up, to Trevor)
OK, I'll fix it. But you stay away from Ford
Granadas, that's the deal for everybody, no
touching the dog's arse and keep your boot out of
the chef's bollocks. Alright?

GILLER comes back into the room.

            GILLER
He's out.

            CLIVE
It doesn't matter, Barry. We're all going to bed,
aren't we, Trevor? Right. Come on, come on, let's
go. Let's go.

TREVOR walks to the door.

            TREVOR
Wankers United!

            GILLER
What happened?

            CLIVE
I'l tell you. Trevor.

TREVOR stops and turns, stares at CLIVE and GILLER

            CLIVE
I don't have to do this, Trevor. I don't have to do
it. Now, if you let me down, Trevor, I'll . . . I'll
kill you – with help, that is. I'll get the chef and
some of the biggest lads I can find, and Wankers
United will bring you down here and, together,
collectively, we'll duff you up, alright?

            TREVOR
Great.

Part Three

Saturday night.

Bangers are old cars taken/donated/purchased from scrap heaps, police lots etc. The interiors of the cars are ripped out, crash and roll bars are fitted, and then they are painted and decorated in bright colours. These cars are then raced round a stadium track until they are bashed or fall to pieces.

Bright lights round the stadium, engines revving, lots of tension. The cars move slowly round the track, bumper to bumper. This is the warm-up lap. Ahead of the racing machines is the control car.

TREVOR is strapped into his vehicle. He's trying to be cool but is considerably hyped up.

At the end of the warm-up lap the control car suddenly accelerates off the track onto the centre island. The cars roar into action and the race is on.

LAPS 2/3/4: TREVOR is just beginning to get a feeling for the race. A large car roars up on the outside and side swipes him as it cuts in to take an inside position. TREVOR is now screaming hell at all around him. He pushes the car into second but, as he begins to accelerate, the car jerks, splutters and dies leaving TREVOR marooned in the centre of the track. TREVOR tries to start the machine but it's dead.

> TREVOR
> Shit! Fuck it. Fuck!

The other cars continue to fight their way round the track. TREVOR is left lost and helpless, a very cold look in his eye. He has no choice but to sit in the dead car while the race roars about him.

Midnight.

A Ford Transit van used by the Centre for day trips etc.
CLIVE, TREVOR and LEROY are on their way back to Hooper
Street. LEROY is 15 years old, black, six foot two.

CLIVE is driving, LEROY sits next to CLIVE, TREVOR sits alone
in a seat at the rear of the van.

> CLIVE
> (to Trevor)
> You were up against professionals, you know,
> nearly all those chaps, those other drivers, they're
> professionals. Men twice your age. Isn't that right,
> Leroy?

> LEROY
> Mmm? Yeah. Yeah.

> CLIVE
> That last race! Like the M1 in fog.
> (he looks at his watch)
> Look at the time. Lie in tomorrow.
> Hey, do you want some fish and chips? Leroy?

> LEROY
> No thanks, had a couple of dogs at the track.

> CLIVE
> If you want to join the project, Trevor, I'll fix it.
> Bloody try, anyway. You're in now, aren't you,
> Leroy?

> LEROY
> Yeah.

> CLIVE
> (to Trevor)
> You could race on a regular basis. Can't be bad,
> can it? Join a team. You wouldn't have to nick cars
> anymore, you'd get them for free. I know they're

free when you nick them, but that's not the point, no, the police donate cars to the project, stolen cars – not ones they've stolen, unclaimed vehicles. Do you want any fish and chips, Trevor?

TREVOR does not respond.

29   Ext. Hooper Street. Night.   29

CLIVE, LEROY and TREVOR walk from the car park to the front entrance of the building, where PETER CLIVE searches his pockets for his large bunch of keys.

> CLIVE
> That's funny, can't find my keys. No. Not here . . . lost them, dropped them –

TREVOR presses the front door bell.

> CLIVE
> Don't press th – too late. Damn. Now we've got Hope or Hopkins on our necks.

> TREVOR
> Heap of fucking tin, that motor, it just died on me.

> LEROY
> Yeah.

CLIVE is still searching his pockets for his keys.

> CLIVE
> I've got a set of dupes somewhere – it's always best with keys.

Sound of the front door being unlocked.

> CLIVE
> Oh, here we go . . .

HOPKINS, night staff, big man, early forties, opens the door. Instant bureaucratic antagonism between CLIVE and HOPKINS.

CLIVE
Hello, Ray –

HOPKINS
What's going on?

CLIVE
Trevor and Leroy have been on a project, Ray,
sorry to distrub you –

HOPKINS
I don't know about this –

CLIVE
Get in, Trevor, Leroy.

HOPKINS
– nobody tells me a thing.

CLIVE
Yes, well, it's in the register, Ray. You should
look.

HOPKINS
As far as I'm concerned this door's locked at ten
thirty p.m.

CLIVE
I'm well aware of that –

HOPKINS locks the front door.

30   Int. Room at Hooper Street. Night.   30

TREVOR and ERROL's room: darkness – and ERROL is asleep.
TREVOR switches on the light. He kicks ERROL's bed, jolts
him awake.

TREVOR
Oi! Oi! Your case conference coming up is it, eh?

                    ERROL
Wha?

                    TREVOR
Watch your lip, watch your fuckin step. Get your
hands off your cock. This one's got a little bit too
much to say for himself, little fucker. Look what I
got.

He holds up PETER CLIVE's bunch of keys.

31   Int. Hooper Street. Night.   31

12:30 a.m.

The dormitory wing.

A bedroom door opens. TREVOR appears. He walks down
the corridor a few paces, sees that the night attendant is not
at his desk, turns and nods to ERROL to follow him.

TREVOR and ERROL walk down the corridor past a room
where GEORGE, the night attendant, is washing his hands
and humming to himself.

32   Int. Records office. Night.   32

An office filled with filing cabinets in which clients' case
notes are stored. Unlocking the door with Clive's keys,
TREVOR and ERROL enter the office.

                    TREVOR
                    (whispering)
            Shut the door. Shut it.

TREVOR switches on the light. ERROL closes the door.
TREVOR checks out the filing cabinets.

                    TREVOR
            What's your name?

                    ERROL
Errol.

                    TREVOR
Other one, prat.

                    ERROL
Duprey.

                    TREVOR
Do – what?

                    ERROL
D-U-P-R-E-Y.

The filing cabinets are locked. TREVOR checks out the bunch
of keys.

                    TREVOR
All these keys, who needs them, eh?

                    ERROL
How'd you get 'em?

                    TREVOR
Clive, the wanker, he dropped them.

He tries a key. It works.

                    ERROL
Where?

                    TREVOR
On the floor.

He opens a filing cabinet which is full of reports and records.

                    TREVOR
D . . . .
          (he sorts through the files)
They got you in here, you little wanker. It's your
file, look. Everything these fuckers have ever said
about you.

ERROL
For my case conference.

TREVOR
Your fucking execution mate. That's your school,
look.

As TREVOR sifts through the documents in the file, he hands
various papers to ERROL.

TREVOR
'Educational Welfare Officer's report'.
'Confidential – report to Juvenile Court. Subject:
Errol Duprey'. 'End of term clinic report'. 'Head of
Year report'. 'Record of school offences: arguing
with the teacher. Disrupting assembly. Kicked
football into staff face from close range'.

ERROL
He kicked me.

TREVOR
'Racist remarks'. Fuckin hell – 'Damaged
calculator by taking it to pieces'.
'Confidential referral form for admission to a
special unit'.

ERROL
I don't know nothing 'bout no special unit.

TREVOR
'My contract by Errol Duprey' – is this your
writing?

ERROL
Yeah, it's the contract.

TREVOR
What you write with – a hammer?

ERROL
A pen.

TREVOR

'I have to behave myself at Hooper Street at all
times. I must obey the staff and teachers at
Hooper Street and if I do go home, I must behave
myself and listen to my mum' – obey the teachers,
listen to your mum – 'I have to be up at eight every
morning and wash and get dressed and have my
breakfast and get ready for school and reach there
at five to nine every morning.' Did you write this
cobblers?

ERROL

They make you do it.

TREVOR

Signed by yours sincerely, Errol Duprey.

ERROL is now holding a bewildering bundle of documents.
TREVOR takes another set of papers from the file.

TREVOR

'Assessment Report on Errol Duprey'. Your case
conference coming up, is it, eh? . . . Can't you
read?

ERROL

Not very well, no.

TREVOR

You fuckin baboon.

TREVOR flips through the pages, reading extracts.

TREVOR

'Attitudes and feelings expressed on admission.
Errol was admitted on a Place of Safety Order, his
mother having rejected him. On admission he was
quiet and well behaved. Later in the week he
became disruptive and moody – his behaviour
proved to be erratic, fluctuating from one moment
to the next.'

ERROL

I don't know what that means. Is that about me?

TREVOR

'Errol has a bright, busy and spontaneous manner, always joking a lot' – that's because he's a fucking monkey – 'He is very imaginative and has an agile mind. He is able to invent situations and role play within them.'

ERROL

What?

TREVOR

'A likeable child, he gets on well with the staff and has a natural aptitude to relate to adults. He often engages in discussions, amusing talks and pitting his wits with members of staff and adults. He can act mature without losing a kind of appropriate childishness. He can often be very affectionate towards male and female members of staff.' Turd burglars, mate, I should watch your arse.

ERROL

I don't know what they're on about. What's it mean?

TREVOR

They're all a load of wankers, mate, that's what it means.

ERROL

Is that supposed to be about me?

TREVOR

'He can be rude and abusive, though.' – thank fuck for that – 'In efforts to have his own way he can become very disruptive. Sporting activities should be made available to him using up excess energy which may otherwise be used in trouble making. Perhaps outward bound activities could be introduced such as camping, hiking and wanking.'

75

ERROL

Is that what it says?

TREVOR flips through yet more papers.

TREVOR

'Psychiatric report. Errol is not suffering from any
form of psychiatric illness' – he's just thick –
'though admits he gets muddled and tearful at
times, particularly if he gets upset by others.' –
what do you expect? – 'The most striking feature
about Errol, at interview, was his nine inch cock' –

ERROL

What?!

TREVOR

– 'was his avowed determination to demand and
have his own way, which undoubtedly leads him
into conflict with adults and peers. He clearly' –

ERROL

Whas peers?

TREVOR

At the seaside. 'He clearly gets very angry if
thwarted in his demands. One suspects that he
could be a powerful anti-authority ring leader in
many settings.'

ERROL

I don't remember saying that. It's all bollocks.
What's going to happen to me, does it say?

TREVOR sifts through the papers, goes back to the
assessment report.

TREVOR

'The future: it seems unlikely for this child to
return home, his mother having rejected him for
her own life style. Bearing this in mind, future
care seems to be the alternative. We would

recommend a care order be made in order to be able to continue our assessment of his needs' – you're in here for life mate.

ERROL is hurt, stung.

>   ERROL
> What'll I do?

>   TREVOR
> Piss on it. Fucking chuck it.

TREVOR chucks Errol's reports over his shoulder onto the floor.

>   TREVOR
> Chuck the fuckin lot of them.

They take reports from the filing cabinet and chuck them onto the office floor.

>   ERROL
> Where's yours?

>   TREVOR
> Who gives a fuck? Bottom drawer. Piss on it.

>   ERROL
> Shit on it.

>   TREVOR
> Fuckin shit on it!

TREVOR pisses onto the reports in the bottom drawer of the filing cabinet while ERROL shits on the reports strewn on the floor.

>   TREVOR
> Fuckin hell, what a stınk!

TREVOR puts out the light.

>   ERROL
> Put it on.

TREVOR looks for a way out of the window – there isn't one.

> ERROL
> I can't see to wipe my arse.

> TREVOR
> Come on.

TREVOR opens the door.

> ERROL
> Wait a minute.

> TREVOR
> Shut it and come on.

They leave the office.

33   Int./Ext. Ford Transit/Car park. Night.   33

TREVOR sorts through the large bunch of assorted car keys, trying different Ford keys in the ignition.

> ERROL
> Come on, man. They'll catch us.

One of the keys connects and the engine roars into life.

> TREVOR
> Easy.

TREVOR reverses the Transit out of the Assessment Centre car park and drives off down the road.

34   Ext. Street. Night.   34

A quiet side street of terraced houses.

The Ford Transit roars down the street and brakes to a standstill.

TREVOR and ERROL get out. They have armed themselves with lumps of concrete and half bricks.

They walk along the street to a house at the end of the terrace.

> TREVOR
> Not that one . . . not that one. Where the fuck is it? Here it is – Mr Shanawankers.

He hurls a brick through the window. They pelt the house with rocks until all the windows are broken. Then they work their way back along the terrace throwing bricks and rocks through the windows of other houses. As they throw the rocks:

> TREVOR
> Fuckin Paki bastards! Get back from where you came from, you fuckin wogs. Dirty black bastards! We don't want you here – get that – Britain is white. Fucking white, white, white! We'll put you in the gas chambers, you baboons. Fuck off back to the Punjab!

> ERROL
> Bastards! Bastards! Fuckin bastards! Fuckin chapatti bastards! Send 'em back! Put 'em on the boats! Black nigger bastards! You baboons! Get back to the jungle!

Lights go on in houses in the street. Faces appear at windows.

> MAN (OOV)
> Oi you. Come back. You hear, come back.

> ERROL
> Come on! They saw us, man.

> TREVOR
> Bollocks.

They get into the Transit.

> ERROL
> They saw us. Look, I don't want no trouble. My case is coming up – lets go back.

They drive off at speed.

A high street with a police station. Parked outside the main entrance to the station is an empty panda patrol car.

The Ford Transit speeds along the high street, pulls in towards the kerb, and bashes to a halt in the back of the patrol car rocketing it forwards onto the kerb.

ERROL is knocked semi-conscious by the impact of the collision.

TREVOR dumps the bunch of keys into ERROL's lap, jumps out of the van, and walks calmly away.

ERROL remains in the van, stunned. Once TREVOR has turned the corner into a side street, he begins to sprint at speed away from the police station.

A POLICEMAN comes out of the police station, followed a few seconds later by a POLICEWOMAN.

The POLICEMAN is stunned by the assault of the large Ford Transit on the innocent panda car – and by the sight of ERROL, who appears to be sitting casually in the front passenger seat of the Transit.

The POLICEMAN goes over to the van and looks in through the window at ERROL.

The POLICEMAN opens the door of the Ford Transit.

>   POLICEMAN
> You little black bastard. Out. Out!

In ERROL's hands are Peter Clive's large bunch of keys which fall to the ground as the POLICEMAN lugs ERROL out of the van. The POLICEMAN picks up the keys and pushes ERROL into the police station.

>   POLICEMAN

Move!

2:00. a.m.
TREVOR strides through a glittering display of secondhand
cars on the forecourt of a large secondhand car dealer.

He takes off his jacket, throws it into the air; it lands on one
of the cars.

A modern shopping precinct. It is deserted, littered with
rubbish from Saturday shoppers.

TREVOR strides through the precinct past brightly lit shop
windows.

He bashes on past the windows of a large general
department store. His eye is caught by one particular display
but he walks on for several yards before he stops and turns
back. He stops at the window and stares at the display.

The display represents the living-room of a British home: a
three-piece suite, a carpet, coffee table, a nest of tables, a
standard lamp and light fittings, pictures on the wall, a
digital clock showing the correct time, a stereo unit, a colour
TV, a video recorder, an Atari TV games attachment – plus
other items.

Seated on the sofa is a window display dummy father,
dressed in casual clothes and holding the TV automatic
control. The dummy father is smiling.

Standing next to a door which leads to a kitchen display in
the next window is a dummy mother. She is holding a tray
which, in turn, holds a tea service.

Standing by the TV is a dummy son. He is dressed in the
uniform of a local school. He is holding an Action Man in full

battle kit, including gas mask. And, under his other arm, he is holding an Action Man tank and an Action Man bazooka.

Lying on its stomach on the carpet, chin in hand, legs crossed in the air, is a dummy daughter. She is holding a Cindy doll in a wedding dress. Next to her, on the carpet, is a Cindy Dresser with make-up etc.

All four dummies are pointing vaguely in the direction of the TV which is showing an automatic rewind video tape of the film 'Lady Caroline Lamb' – a costume drama about the English upper-classes.

There is a price tag on every single item in the display.

TREVOR stares at the family, soaking in all the details.

Then he cuts out and moves off with even greater determination. He begins to sprint.

> TREVOR
> (from the gut)
> Bollocks!

He runs towards the exit of the precinct.

39   Ext. Tunnel. Night.   39

The Blackwall Tunnel. Bright lights reflect off the tiles of the tunnel walls.

TREVOR strides along like a soldier on a route march. A mass of energy pumping through him. He peels off his T-shirt and throws it to the ground.

An oncoming vehicle hoots its horn at TREVOR. TREVOR kicks at the vehicle as it drives by and screams at the DRIVER.

> TREVOR
> Wanker! Wanker! Fuckin wanker!

40   Ext. Side street. Night.   40

TREVOR strides along a side street. He stops and looks through a spiked iron fence into the playground of Bradley Street School where he was once a pupil. Then straight on, past the locked school gates.

41   Ext. House. Night.   41

Just before dawn.

TREVOR stands in the middle of the road staring at one particular house which contains HARRY PARKER's second floor flat.

At the front door: two rows of lit-up push buttons with the residents' names written on them. TREVOR presses the buttons at random. Confusion as a babel of voices speak back through the Ansaphone.

>   PARKER
>   (On the Ansaphone)
>   Alright, alright. Second floor, Come up.

A buzzer sounds to indicate the door is unlocked. TREVOR enters the building.

On his way up the stairs he passes a confused WOMAN in her dressing gown.

>   TREVOR
>   Oi, oi, you up early missus?

He raps on her front door.

When he reaches the second floor he passes one of the men woken by his bell ringing. It is MR DRIVER, an elderly gentleman, standing in his doorway.

>   TREVOR
>   (belches loudly)
>   What you looking at?

MR DRIVER
Just a minute. Hey, excuse me –

PARKER
I'm sorry about that Mr Driver.

HARRY PARKER is dressed in trousers and a T-shirt. He is not pleased to see TREVOR. Another RESIDENT appears, disturbed by the noise.

PARKER
(to the other resident)
I'm sorry, John. I thought it was the taxi for the airport. I'm sorry.

TREVOR goes into PARKER's flat. PARKER closes the door.

42   Int. Flat. Night.   42

The PARKERs' flat: suitcases are piled up at the front door, ready for the family's departure to the airport for their holiday.

TREVOR takes in the suitcases. He knows the PARKERS are about to go on holiday.

PARKER
(to Trevor)
You nurd!

TREVOR
You going away, Harry?

PARKER
In there – keep your voice down.

They go into the living-room.

TREVOR
You going on holiday, Harry?

PARKER
What do you want, Trevor? What's going on?

TREVOR
I'm turning myself in.

MRS PARKER
(from the bedroom)
Harry.

PARKER
What do you mean?

MRS PARKER
Harry.

PARKER
Wait there and don't make a noise.

PARKER goes into the bedroom.

TREVOR instantly noses around and finds his way into the children's bedroom.

The Parkers' two children, TERRY and ANNIE, are fast asleep. ANNIE is eight years old and TERRY twelve years old.

There are Tottenham FC posters and mementos on the wall.

TREVOR stares at the boy, TERRY, just four years his junior.

PARKER, having failed to find TREVOR in the living-room, stands in the doorway of the bedroom. TREVOR does not notice him.

PARKER
Oi.

TREVOR
(pointing to the Tottenham mementos)
Up the Yids.

PARKER
Out.

TREVOR follows PARKER into the living-room.

PARKER

You wake him up and I'll boot your arse. I didn't go to bed 'til one and I'm up again at six. I've had bugger all sleep, so watch it, right? Now, what's going on?

TREVOR

I had a bust up with those wankers you put me with.

PARKER

Where you put yourself, Trevor, not me. I kept you out of there for bloody months.

TREVOR

You're pissing off on your holidays.

PARKER

If you can't keep straight for two weeks in the year, you're not worth a toss. Now when did you bunk off?

TREVOR

About one.

PARKER

Tonight?

TREVOR

Yeah.

PARKER

Then take my advice and bunk back in, before it's too late.

TREVOR

I bust the Job Centre window.

PARKER

What? When?

TREVOR

Friday.

PARKER
But I only took you in there Thursday.

TREVOR
They don't know I did it.

PARKER
The Assessment Centre?

TREVOR
Yeah.

PARKER
But you're telling me.

TREVOR
(with a smile)
Yeah.

PARKER
Great.

TERRY PARKER stands in the bedroom doorway.

TERRY
Is it time yet, dad?

PARKER
No, not yet, Terry, I'll tell you when it's time to
go.

TERRY stares at TREVOR.

TREVOR
Hello, Tel.

PARKER
Back to bed . . . I'm working. Now, come on.

TERRY goes back to bed. PARKER is cool, ready to commit
murder.

TREVOR
I nicked the Transit from the Centre.

PARKER

When?

TREVOR

Tonight.

PARKER

What else?

TREVOR

Me and Errol chucked bricks through
Mr Shanawanker's window.

ANNIE calls from the bedroom.

ANNIE

Mum!

PARKER

Shit!

ANNIE

Mum!

TERRY

Mum, Annie wants to go to the toilet.

PARKER goes to the door and calls his wife.

PARKER

Viv!

MRS PARKER
(from the bedroom)

Alright.

MRS PARKER gets up and takes ANNIE to the lavatory.

PARKER

Mr Who – whose windows?

TREVOR

That Paki bastard who had me put away.

PARKER
What about Harrods' windows – you do them too?

TREVOR
I didn't think of that.

PARKER
Who's . . . who's Errol?

TREVOR
A nig-nog from the Centre. I dumped him in the
Transit at the Police Station. I turned him in.

PARKER
Is that all?

TREVOR
Yeah. Oh no. I pissed on my files – in the Centre.
Errol shit on his. I'm turning myself in to you,
Harry, as you're my mate you can collect the
reward.

PARKER
Where did you leave Errol and the Transit? What
police station?

PARKER goes over to the telephone where he picks up his
address book.

TREVOR
One near Bradley Street School.

PARKER looks up the number in his book.

PARKER
Crapping on your own doorstep.

PARKER finds the number.

PARKER
We'll let them deal with it.

He dials, then stops to listen to TREVOR.

TREVOR
They'll stand on me, Harry. They don't like me
there, I been there before. They'll roll me in a
mattress and boot me.

PARKER
What's that to a brick shithouse like you?

PARKER re-dials the number of the police station.

TREVOR
I smashed a police car with a Transit. Send me to
another nick.

PARKER
Your shit, you roll in it.

PARKER looks at TREVOR.

PARKER
You're an arsehole Trevor, you're not worth a
piss.

TREVOR smiles.

TREVOR
Right – like my file.

43   Int. A cell. Night.   43

In the cell there is a place for TREVOR to lie down, but no
blankets or covers. There is a toilet which flushes from the
outside of the cell.

It is cold. TREVOR is still stripped to the waist. He has his
finger on the buzzer which calls the DUTY POLICEMAN.

The DUTY POLICEMAN opens the small 'viewing window',
but does not unlock the door.

POLICEMAN
Take your finger off that bleedin buzzer.

TREVOR stands at the door and looks through at the POLICEMAN on the other side.

> POLICEMAN
> What do you want?

> TREVOR
> Can you flush the toilet, I dun a crap.

The POLICEMAN slams shut the window and walks back down the corridor. TREVOR still stands with his face close to the door. He reflects for a few seconds.

TREVOR walks over to the cell window and then over to the bell. He leans his head against the buzzer.

44   Int. Corridor. Night.   44

The same POLICEMAN plus PC ANSON walk down the corridor. The POLICEMAN opens the cell door and they both go into the cell.

45   Int. Cell. Night.   45

Both POLICEMEN are young, not much older than TREVOR.

> POLICEMAN
> Now I told you to keep your hand off that buzzer.

> TREVOR
> I'm a juvenile offender, you can't keep me in a cell.
>   (to Anson)
> I know you.

> PC ANSON
> Do you?

> TREVOR
> I've been charged now, you can't keep me in a cell. You got to send me back to the Assessment Centre.

PC ANSON
Shut your mouth, will you? Just shut it.

TREVOR
You gotta look after me, give me something to eat.

PC ANSON produces a truncheon.

PC ANSON
You see this? Sit down and shut your fuckin
rabbit.

TREVOR
(remembers the policeman's name)
PC Anson.

PC ANSON
Shut it.

TREVOR sits down.

PC ANSON
You're straight into Court Monday, and you ain't
going back to no Assessment Centre. You're going
straight to a Detention Centre, or borstal. And
when you come out we are going to be waiting
outside the gate for you, and we're going to put
you in a car and we're going to bring you straight
back down here and we're going to take your
finger prints. We can't do that now, juvenile
offender, but once you've been to a DC or borstal,
we can screw you. And we will. We got you now,
and once we've got your finger prints we're going
to do you for every unsolved taking and driving
away in this district, stretching back over months –
and that's a lot of cars, I can tell you – and you'll
go down and you'll stay down. For years. We'll
see to that.

TREVOR
Sounds great.

PC ANSON hits TREVOR on the knee with his truncheon.
TREVOR almost vomits with pain.

> PC ANSON
> You think you're hard, don't you? A lot of verbals.
> There's two things you're going to learn. At home,
> at school, at work, in the street, you will respect
> authority and you will obey the rules, just like
> everybody else – that's discipline. Most kids know
> that by the time they reach your age. Shut it and
> keep it shut.

The TWO POLICEMEN leave the cell. The door slams, the lock
hits home. TREVOR grits his teeth into a smile.

46   Ext. Detention Centre. Day.   46

At first view, the DC gives the impression of being an
English public school. There is a large period house set in its
own mature grounds – just the kind of place one would go
for an educational weekend course.

A series of shots show the grounds with its beautiful trees,
shrubs, neat borders and impeccably manicured lawns.

The house is extremely well maintained, no expense has
been spared to keep the paintwork crisp and the windows
gleaming.

It is the incongruous intrusive appearance of an extremely
high chain-link fence into this pleasant landscape which tells
us we are not in an English public school but a place of
detention.

A detachment of INMATES, flanked by WARDERS on either
side, march in crisp formation down the main drive towards
the front of the house.

It is raining.

To the rear of the house, there is a large expanse of open ground. The ground is wet and muddy from the heavy downpour of rain.

There is a group of YOUTHS, black and white, strung out in a line across this expanse of mud. Armed with forks and spades, they are digging the ground. Using the trench-digging technique, they are cutting out large sods of heavy wet earth and turning them over.

TREVOR is in the centre, digging hard and fast. The YOUTH next to TREVOR is finding it very hard going; he is on the point of giving up. TREVOR urges him on.

>   TREVOR
>   (smashing his spade into the earth)
> Come on . . . come on, you bastard.
> . . . This is great, fuckin great.
> This is how they train the creme de la creme.
> Bleeding storm troopers. SS. SAS. Heroes of the
> nation. That's us. Brick shithouses. Doors off
> hinges. Dig, you bastard!

>   WARDER
>   (from the end of the line)
> You! Watch your mouth! Keep it shut!

>   TREVOR
>   (goes on talking)
> Dig you bastard! Dig! We've got the buggers on
> the run. It's our fucking turn!

TREVOR slices deep into the earth with his spade.

Music.

Cut in title:

>   MADE IN BRITAIN

Appendix

The list below gives all but the very minor differences between the text in this book and the broadcast version of the film. The following passages are *not* found in the broadcast version.

Scene 5. PARKER: 'You have just . . . Social Services.'
TREVOR: 'You didn't help' *to* PARKER: 'wanking, mate.'
Scene 6. PARKER: 'You'll be alright . . . if you're lucky.'

Scene 32. TREVOR: 'Attitudes and feelings' *to* ERROL: 'does it say?'
Scenes 46 and 47. All.

UK82 – The Exploited:

Violence starts upon the street
and Thatcher wonders why.
Is this life in '82?
I know I'd rather die.

Hit them hard and hit them fast
Those that say you cannot pass
You're a free man not a slave
Show them you're not afraid.

We're just a nation under stress
We're really in a fucking mess,
Instead of being better off
We cope with less and less.

You studied bloody hard at school
You played the game with its golden rules.
What did you find once you left
No future for social rejects.